THE BELL WITCH

AN AMERICAN GHOST STORY

—◦◦◦ BY MEGAN COOLEY PETERSON ◦◦◦—

CAPSTONE PRESS
a capstone imprint

Snap Books are published by Capstone Press
1710 Roe Crest Drive, North Mankato, Minnesota 56003
www.capstonepub.com

Library of Congress Cataloging-in-Publication Data is available on the Library of Congress website.

ISBNs:
978-1-5435-7335-0 (hardcover)
978-1-5435-7477-7 (paperback)
978-1-5435-7344-2 (eBook PDF)

Editorial Credits
Eliza Leahy, editor; Brann Garvey, designer; Tracy Cummins, media researcher; Tori Abraham, production specialist

Photo Credits
Alamy: age fotostock, 8, Trinity Mirror/Mirrorpix, 15; Courtesy of Tennessee State Library and Archives: 6, 17, 24; Shutterstock: ADragan, 23, Africa Studio, 18, avtk, Design Element, Bob Orsillo, 11, Chantal de Bruijne, Design Element, Everett Historical, 21, Giraphics, Design Element, GoMixer, Design Element, Hitdelight, 9, InnaPoka, 7, Joe Therasakdhi, Cover, LiskaM, 13, Lusica, 19, MagicDogWorkshop, Design Element, NikhomTreeVector, Design Element, NinaMalyna (frame), 9 Top, 21, 24, Prokrida (frame), 9 Left, 9 Bottom, Stefan Rotter, 12; Wikimedia: Brian Stansberry, 5, 27, Www78, 29

Direct Quotations
Pages 14–15: Ingram, M.V. *An Authenticated History of the Famous Bell Witch*. Clarksville, TN: W. P. Titus, printer, 1894, 53.
Page 20: Ingram, M.V. *An Authenticated History of the Famous Bell Witch*. Clarksville, TN: W. P. Titus, printer, 1894, 57–58.
Page 23: Ingram, M.V. *An Authenticated History of the Famous Bell Witch*. Clarksville, TN: W. P. Titus, printer, 1894, 91.

TABLE OF CONTENTS

AFRAID OF THE DARK

The Bell family from Adams, Tennessee, feared the dark. From 1817 to 1821, a **poltergeist** haunted the family every night. It pulled their hair and overturned furniture. It threw back bedsheets and choked the children. The ghost, nicknamed the Bell Witch, even **allegedly** killed one member of the Bell family.

The Bells were, by all accounts, a normal family. John and Lucy married in 1782 and had nine children. The family attended church and school. They were friendly with their neighbors. So what made this ghost haunt them? And was there really a ghost at all? Some **skeptics** believe the Bells invented the ghost for attention. Other people believe the haunting actually occurred.

The Bell log cabin is the only original structure that still exists from the Bells' farm. The Bell family used it as an outbuilding.

CHAPTER ONE

THE TROUBLE BEGINS

In 1804, John and Lucy Bell and their children moved from North Carolina to Tennessee. They had heard of the area's rich farmland and dense forests. They purchased property on the Red River, which included a house and barns. John cleared some of the land and started farming. Life in Tennessee seemed perfect.

Until the trouble began.

The Bell homestead sat on the Red River. The fertile land was perfect for farming.

It was the summer of 1817. While working in the field, John stumbled upon a strange animal sitting between two rows of corn. It looked like a dog with the head of a rabbit. John raised his gun and shot at the creature, but it ran off.

The strange sightings didn't end there. A few days later, John and Lucy's son Drew spotted a large turkey perched on a fence. As Drew approached the bird, he saw that it wasn't a turkey at all. The bird flapped its large wings and took off. Drew had no idea what kind of bird it might be.

Betsy, the youngest daughter, went for a walk in the woods near the house around this same time. She saw a girl in a green dress climbing one of the oak trees. She had never seen this girl before and found it strange.

A few days later, one of the Bells' **enslaved** workers reported seeing a large, black dog in the road. This dog followed him every night when he went to visit his wife. She was also enslaved and lived with a different family. As soon as the man arrived at his wife's door each night, the dog ran away.

Little did the Bells know, these odd events were about to take a terrifying turn.

WITCHES
AND FAMILIARS

Is it possible that the Bells' strange animal sightings had something to do with the **paranormal**? According to **folklore**, witches had animals called "familiars." These animals could assist a witch in her magical workings. A familiar could spy on people, steal from them, and even attack them. Black cats were said to be favored by witches. But other animals could also serve as familiars, such as toads, dogs, and other small animals.

CHAPTER TWO

UNSEEN HANDS

Members of the Bell family didn't think much of the strange creatures they'd seen around the farm. But then one night, strange scratching and banging sounds began outside the house. The family went outside to **investigate**, and the sounds stopped. Each night as the family went to bed, the scratching and banging started. And each time they went outside, the sounds were replaced with silence.

The strange sounds soon moved inside the house, starting in the boys' bedroom. A sound like rats gnawing on the bedposts woke the boys. The two eldest sons, John Jr. and Drew, got up to kill the rats. But as soon as their feet hit the floor, the gnawing stopped. They looked under the beds and found no rats or chew marks. Once the brothers climbed back into bed, the gnawing started again. The boys stayed up half the night searching for the source of the gnawing.

SKEPTIC'S NOTE

Scratching sounds can be caused by tree branches moving in the wind or animals crawling around the house.

ii

The gnawing sounds continued for weeks, now in all the bedrooms. The Bells also heard dogs fighting and the sound of chains being dragged across the floor. Whenever someone lit a candle, the sounds ceased.

The family examined every room in the house. They moved furniture and pulled up rugs. But no one could find the source of the nightly **racket**. It steadily grew worse. Along with the gnawing, the Bell family heard lips smacking and the sound of someone choking. The noises stopped every night between one and three in the morning.

JOHN BELL'S ILLNESS

John Bell began to experience some strange health problems around this time. His tongue would swell up in his mouth. Sometimes he was unable to eat. John said it felt as if a small piece of wood had been lodged sideways in his mouth, pushing at his cheeks.

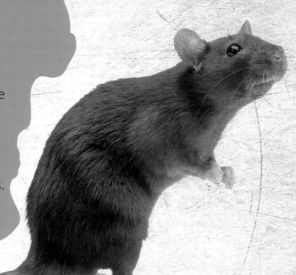

A TERRIFYING TURN

After about a year, the strange sounds turned into poltergeist-like activity. One night, 6-year-old Richard Williams had just fallen asleep. Suddenly it felt as though someone was twisting his hair. Unseen hands pulled so hard he was lifted right out of bed. "It felt like the top of my head had been taken off," he later recalled. Something also pulled Betsy's hair. Covers were torn off beds while the family slept.

John and Lucy had no idea what was causing the paranormal activity. They began staying up all night to protect their children. They decided to invite their neighbors Dr. James Johnson and his wife to spend the night in their home. They wanted someone outside the family to witness the events.

Before bedtime, James read some passages from the Bible. He also prayed that the Bell family would no longer be haunted. Despite the prayer, the activity started up as soon as everyone went to bed. Chairs overturned, and covers flew off beds.

James tried speaking with the **entity**. "In the name of the Lord, what or who are you? What do you want and why are you here?" he asked. But the entity wouldn't answer. James concluded it had to be some kind of spirit. But what did it want with the Bell family?

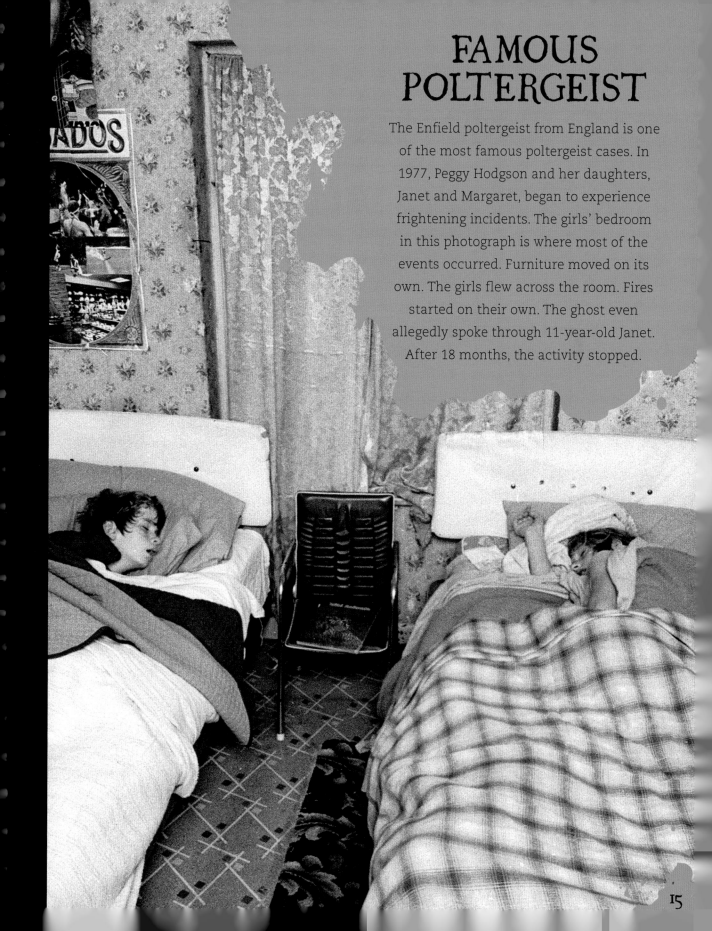

FAMOUS POLTERGEIST

The Enfield poltergeist from England is one of the most famous poltergeist cases. In 1977, Peggy Hodgson and her daughters, Janet and Margaret, began to experience frightening incidents. The girls' bedroom in this photograph is where most of the events occurred. Furniture moved on its own. The girls flew across the room. Fires started on their own. The ghost even allegedly spoke through 11-year-old Janet. After 18 months, the activity stopped.

CHAPTER THREE

THE GHOST TARGETS BETSY BELL

The ghost soon set its sights on another family member—Betsy. Betsy's cheeks turned red from being slapped by the ghost. Sometimes Betsy couldn't breathe. It felt as if someone was choking her. She also felt as though something was sticking her with sharp pins. Her hair comb would be ripped from her head and tossed to the ground. A woman's laughter could be heard, as if it took joy in Betsy's pain. They assumed the voice belonged to the ghost.

SKEPTIC'S NOTE

Betsy's hair comb could have simply fallen out. The family was already on edge. They might have blamed normal, everyday occurrences on the ghost.

Betsy's parents were terrified the ghost might try to kill their daughter. They sent her to her friends' houses to sleep, hoping the ghost wouldn't follow. But it **harassed** Betsy no matter where she slept.

This drawing of Betsy Bell was first published in 1894 in *An Authenticated History of the Bell Witch* by M. V. Ingram.

A PRESIDENTIAL GHOST HUNTER?

In the summer of 1819, word of the Bell Witch reached future U.S. president Andrew Jackson. According to legend, Jackson came to the farm to investigate for himself. Within a mile of the farm, Jackson's wagon wheels locked up. Jackson blamed the event on the Bell Witch. The spirit answered that it was responsible and let the wagon continue. At the house, one of his men bragged that he could kill the witch. The witch lifted the man and tossed him about the house.

BAD MEDICINE

Betsy became desperate to rid herself of the ghost. A doctor came to the house, claiming he could cure her. He had mixed up a special medicine for her to drink. Betsy's friend Theny Thorn advised her against it, but she drank it anyway.

Within moments of taking the medicine, Betsy vomited. Theny noticed something strange about what she had thrown up. Upon closer **examination**, the vomit was full of pins and needles. The ghost laughed as Theny cleaned up the mess. Everyone agreed the ghost must have dropped the pins and needles into the vomit when no one was looking. No one, it seemed, could cure Betsy of her troubles.

SKEPTIC'S NOTE

Either Betsy or Theny could have dropped the pins into the mess when the other wasn't looking.

FACT

Theny collected some of the pins and needles and kept them for the rest of her life.

Some people suggested that perhaps Betsy was the cause of the strange occurrences. She may have been making the whole thing up for attention. But that **theory** ended when the ghost began speaking. At first it only whistled when asked a question. Then the ghost began to speak in a low whisper. "I am the spirit of a person who was buried in the woods nearby," the ghostly voice said. "The grave has been disturbed, my bones **disinterred** and scattered, and one of my teeth was lost under this house, and I am here looking for that tooth."

As the family searched the house for a lost tooth, the ghost cackled with glee. It said it was all a joke to fool John, whom the ghost called Old Jack. The Bell Witch also took an interest in Betsy's boyfriend, Joshua Gardner. The ghost would whisper at Betsy in a hushed voice not to marry Joshua. No one could figure out why the ghost disliked Joshua.

FACT

The Bell Witch haunting inspired the horror movie *The Blair Witch Project*.

SIMILARITIES TO THE SALEM WITCH TRIALS

In 1692 and 1693, 19 people were found guilty of **witchcraft** and hanged in Salem, Massachusetts. Like the Bell Witch haunting, the activity centered around young girls. They spoke in strange voices. Unseen hands pinched and bit them. Their bodies contorted. The girls mainly accused women of using witchcraft against them. One of the men accused, Giles Corey, refused to continue with his trial. He was tortured to death. After the trials, one accuser admitted to making the whole thing up.

More than 200 people were accused of witchcraft during the Salem Witch Trials.

CHAPTER FOUR

A DEADLY END

The year was 1820, and the Bell family had experienced three years of unexplained **phenomena**. For most of this time, John Bell suffered discomfort in his mouth. But as the years wore on, his pain grew steadily worse. The swelling in his mouth became so severe that he couldn't talk or eat for 10 or 15 hours at a time. The muscles in his face began to **contort**, and he was often too sick to get out of bed. Oddly, as John's symptoms grew worse, Betsy's improved.

On the morning of December 19, John did not wake up at his usual time. When the family could not wake him, John Jr. went to the medicine cabinet. Inside, he found a strange **vial** containing dark liquid. No one had ever seen this vial before. "It's useless for you to try to revive Old Jack," the ghost said. "I have got him this time; he will never get up from that bed again." The ghostly voice also admitted that it had fed John the medicine.

FACT

The Bell Witch allegedly adored Lucy Bell and never bothered her.

This image, showing the scene of John Bell's death, was published in M. V. Ingram's 1894 account of the Bell Witch haunting.

FACT

A bit of the strange medicine was given to a cat. Within moments of drinking the liquid, the cat supposedly died.

The doctor soon arrived at the Bell house. He had never seen the vial before either. John's breath reeked of the medicine. When the doctor tossed the vial into the fire, a bright blue haze shot up the chimney. On December 20, 1820, John Bell died. His official cause of death: poisoning.

A few months after John's death, the Bell Witch told the family it would return in seven years. As promised, the ghost allegedly returned to the Bell farm in February 1828. According to Richard Williams, the witch started up with her old behavior. She scratched the bed posts and snatched off covers.

The Bell Witch claimed she would return in 1935 to visit John Bell's closest relative, but there is no proof she ever did. After about two or three weeks, the ghost vanished.

CHAPTER FIVE

WHO WAS THE BELL WITCH?

No one knows for sure who the Bell Witch was. At the time of the haunting, many people blamed a local woman named Kate Batts. They believed she was a witch. Kate owned a farm near the Bells. She and John allegedly had a disagreement when the Bells first moved into the area, and Kate was said to have cursed John Bell.

Another theory is that the Bell Witch was a poltergeist. Some paranormal experts believe a poltergeist isn't a ghost at all. These experts say that an individual can cause a ghostlike disturbance using only their minds. This person might be going through physical or emotional stress and not realize they're causing the activity.

FACT

After Lucy Bell died, no one ever lived in the Bell house again. It was eventually torn down.

TENNESSEE CIVIL WAR TRAILS

3C   38

BELL WITCH

To the north was the farm of John Bell, an early, prominent settler from North Carolina. According to legend, his family was harried during the early 19th century by the famous Bell Witch. She kept the household in turmoil, assaulted Bell, and drove off Betsy Bell's suitor. Even Andrew Jackson who came to investigate, retreated to Nashville after his coach wheels stopped mysteriously. Many visitors to the house saw the furniture crash about them and heard her shriek, sing, and curse.

TENNESSEE HISTORICAL COMMISSION

This historic marker in Adams tells a brief history of the hauntings the Bell family endured.

Could someone in or close to the family have faked the haunting? Some suggest a man named Richard Powell did just that. Powell was a teacher who knew the Bell family. He wanted to marry Betsy, but she was already dating Joshua Gardner. Some say he made up the haunting to scare Joshua away. Betsy did eventually marry Powell.

More than 200 years after the haunting began, the story of the Bell Witch continues to captivate audiences. We'll never know for sure who—or what—caused the ghostlike activity that haunted the Bell family. But it can be fun to guess.

A FAKED MANUSCRIPT?

Richard Williams Bell allegedly wrote about his experiences with the witch almost 30 years after they happened. His account was included in *An Authenticated History of the Famous Bell Witch* by M.V. Ingram. But Richard Williams's original manuscript has never been found. Some believe Ingram made it up.

GLOSSARY

allegedly (uh-LEDGE-id-lee)—said to be true or to have happened, but without proof

contort (kuhn-TORT)—to twist into strange positions

disinterred (dis-in-TERD)—dug up something that was buried

enslaved (in-SLAYVED)—a person who is enslaved is forced to be the legal property of another person and to obey him or her

entity (EN-tuh-tee)—something that exists by itself and is separate from other things

examination (ig-ZAM-uh-NAY-shuhn)—a careful check

folklore (FOHK-lor)—tales, sayings, and customs among a group of people

harassed (huh-RAST)—bothered someone again and again

investigate (in-VES-ti-gate)—gather information about something

paranormal (pair-uh-NOR-muhl)—having to do with an event that has no scientific explanation

phenomenon (fe-NOM-uh-non)—a very unusual or remarkable event

poltergeist (POHL-tur-guyst)—a ghost that causes physical events, such as objects moving

racket (RAK-it)—a lot of noise

skeptic (SKEP-tik)—someone who doubts or questions beliefs

theory (THEER-ee)—an idea or opinion based on some facts but not proven

vial (VYE-uhl)—a very small glass or plastic container used for medicines or perfumes

witchcraft (WICH-kraft)—the practice of magic

READ MORE

Dyer, Janice. *Haunted Woods and Caves*. Haunted or Hoax? New York: Crabtree Publishing Company, 2018.

Gagne, Tammy. *Famous Ghosts*. Ghosts and Hauntings. North Mankato, MN: Capstone Press, 2019.

Giannini, Alex. *Frightening Farmhouses*. Scary Places. New York: Bearport Publishing, 2019.

INTERNET SITES

All about Ghosts:
https://kids.britannica.com/students/article/ghost/311403

The Bell Witch Cave:
https://www.atlasobscura.com/places/the-bell-witch-cave-adams-tennessee

The Truth behind Ghost Stories:
https://www.npr.org/2013/10/27/240824786/the-truth-that-creeps-beneath-our-spooky-ghost-stories

INDEX